Return of the Wolf

Return
of the Wolf

Martin Bell

THE SEABURY PRESS
NEW YORK

1983
The Seabury Press
815 Second Avenue
New York, N.Y. 10017

Printed in the United States of America

Library of Congress Cataloging in Publication Data

Bell, Martin.
 Return of the wolf.

 1. Meditations.   I. Title.
BV4832.2.B4   1983   248.4   83-11549
ISBN 0-8164-0545-X
ISBN 0-8164-2470-5 (pbk.)

Every now and then, I think about dedicating
something to Robert Blake—because I like his
acting and because I like what he has to say.
He doesn't know it, but he made my life possible
when the way was getting pretty dark. All things
considered, this is probably as good a time as
any to tell him thanks. And since it's unlikely
he would ever sit still for a lengthy tribute,
I'll make it a one-liner:

To Robert Blake

For salvation is nearer to us now
than when we first believed;
the night is far gone,
the day is at hand.

Romans 13:11–12

Contents

Return of the Wolf

Prologue

Before there was anything, there was nothing. The Story told of nothing. A great bearded legend stalking about in emptiness, the Story was not something. Cosmic dimensions were not. The eternal came from nowhere. There were no hopes. No dreams. No aspirations. Life and death had yet to be.

Spinning, whirling, crushing vortex of God, the Story was not lonely. The legend was not new. From nothing arose energy. From void came forth what never was. Imagine the power of God without thunder, the majesty of God as Story, as fable, utterly fabulous. Tell the Story of no-time, no-space, no-thing, no-one, "no-body.

Out of nothing came time. And space erupted in the first somewhere. Space-time became duration. Thus the Story had a beginning. Now also it could continue, it could end. Imagine the power of God at the dawn of creation—eternal legend permeating the matrix of historical situation. All as it was intended, to be sure. Nevertheless, *for the first time*, the Story was lonely, and afraid.

Ursula and
the Nighthawk

Ursula was a fine little girl. No one had anything disparaging to say about her. Except for Kevin, and he was an unpleasant child, at best. She called her mother Marguerite by invitation, but never once called her father Chad, since Chad preferred that she call him Father. Although she did not have any brothers or sisters, Ursula had many friends from school, and got along well with the children in her neighborhood. When she was five years old, she had been bitten by Mr. Lichfield's Doberman—but all of that was in the past. Now she was a kind and healthy eight-year-old and her parents were very proud indeed.

At first the hawk only came at night. Through an open window it flew into her bedroom and began to circle. "Ursula, Ursula, I am Gretchen, friend of children. Come and play with me."

"No," said the little girl. "You are not my friend. You are a frightening bird."

The hawk seemed to hover in midair, still flapping its wings. "Frightening bird? Why yes, that's right. Oh yes, frightening bird. I am Gretchen, friend of children."

Mighty Gretchen, fierce protector of all children,
Intercede for us.
The tunnel is dark—
The way is perilous.
Tomorrow rises out of the ashes of today,
Minute by minute the past mysteriously becomes
        present,
And we are afraid.
Persistent friend of children who suffer,
Pray for us.
Creation shifts imperceptibly,
And life is nurtured by death.
Guardian hawk,
Comfort those in your charge.

Growing up is a totally precarious business. It must never be taken for granted. Ursula reached fifteen years of age by sheer grace. She was not hit by a bus. And she did not contract a crippling or fatal disease. Miraculously, she squeaked by. So did Kevin.

Ursula never told anyone about Gretchen. She continued going to school, there absorbing the value system of her social environment. Beneath the mass of data presented as *fact*, she found hidden lessons—obedience, punctuality, moderation, and security. Kevin learned all of this too. And he became far less unpleasant. Curiously, Ursula wondered whether she liked him as much as before.

"You're very unpleasant, Gretchen," Ursula said to the hawk.

"Friend of children," Gretchen replied.

"But I am no longer a child."

Head cocked, the hawk stared at Ursula. "Come and play with me."

"Oh, Gretchen, don't say that. You are still my friend, but I can't come and play now. Don't you understand?"

"No," said Gretchen softly. "Friend of children I am."

Radiant Gretchen, primordial messenger of the
  Divine,
Shatter our worldly values.
Though the future can build only on what has yet
  occurred,
It is we who choose the past.
Drive us therefore to the abyss of holy insecurity—
Free us to be consumed.
Fierce protector of all children everywhere,
Confront us with life.
A fire blazes and leaps forth,
Then is extinguished.
Frightful advocate,
Do not spare us this destiny.

Hawklike in appearance, hair streaked with gray, Ursula walked slowly down a corridor of the children's psychiatric unit. Impatient young doctors, some of them brilliant, were waiting—she seldom was on time for anything. Inside one sunlit room, Kimberly struggled with several building blocks.

"Hello, Dr. Ursula," she called.

"So Kimberly," Ursula said, stopping by the door-
way. "What are you doing?"

"I'm making a rhinoceros for my mother."

"A rhinoceros, is it?"

"A *big* rhinoceros!"

"Good. Yes, that's a perfect idea. A big one is
better, eh?"

"Big!"

"O.K. You make the rhinoceros and I will be back
to see it. First I must teach, then I will see the rhinoc-
eros."

"You won't forget?"

"No, Kimberly, I won't forget."

Ursula smiled and walked away toward the class-
room. She paused momentarily, then shoved both hands
into the pockets of her wrinkled white coat and pushed
the swinging door open with one shoulder. Never did
she look at the class, or use the chalkboard. Addressing
her full attention to an old oak tree outside the window,
she began to speak. "Again, may I remind all of you to
disregard academic considerations. Forget that you are
doctors of medicine. Here, only one thing matters. There
is a single imperative. Be a friend of children. . . ."

Luminous Gretchen, word-bearing hawk of
        everlasting inescapability,
Enable our broken lives.
The passage is narrow
That leads into the darkness of our center.
Purpose springs forth from becoming,
And insight is born in unavoidable encounter with
        mysterious not-yet.

Dangerous intruder from another realm,
Reforge our spirits.
Moment by moment, life is expended.
We hold out before us the awesome questions of how
and where.
Fierce protector of all children who struggle to
understand,
Intercede for us.

In the years that followed, many children were
healed, many were not. The odds against which Ursula
fought were staggering. From time to time, colleagues
suggested that her passion was excessive. That she
became too involved in the lives of her children. That
she did not understand the value of moderation. Some
called her eccentric, even insane. Others spoke of her
as an absolute genius. But whatever the assessment, it
was impossible to ignore her. When teaching, Ursula
never answered questions, and she never gave exami-
nations. Her students were expected to learn whatever
they could, then give themselves a grade. One year,
three physicians gave up psychiatric residency because
of her. It was as if the woman were not of this world.
She seemed driven by some unearthly vision.

Whereas nothing in the natural order of things
suggests a realm beyond that which is perceived, nev-
ertheless many people continue to be motivated by
hope, enabled by love, and sustained by faith. So it was
with Ursula. She knew the ravages of this world all too
well—children physically and psychically abused, tor-
tured, abandoned, raped. She worked and played with
children who were severely retarded, autistic, and

schizophrenic. Moreover, Ursula also understood the devastating truth about healing. It was not hers to bestow. It happened or it didn't. The one Gretchen had singled out many years ago could do so little, other than *be* who she was—Ursula, friend of children.

Of course, there is always a catch. Just when our spirits have matured a little, our bodies usually give out. God alone knows where we have come from or what our final destiny will be. But on the journey within time, invariably we return to the place from which we began.

Unfailing Gretchen, destinal mediator of infinite
*   possibility,*
Strengthen our souls unto the end.
Time returns to no-time.
Utter vulnerability remains.
There is a mystery at the core of life
Which partakes of eternal purpose and temporal
*   existence.*
Divine messenger of painful acknowledgment and
*   absolute risk,*
Confront us with finitude.
The veil of the temple is torn asunder,
A child cries out and shepherds tremble.
Faithful enabler,
Give courage to your children.

How frail she looked sitting there, flesh so thin, eyes sunken deep, balding but for a few stubborn wisps of uncombed hair. Eighty-seven years of human individuality, strapped into a brightly-colored highchair, Ursula stared vacantly at the crowded hall. Dark stains on her bib bore silent witness to the difficulty with which food was taken. Misshapen, uncoordinated hands clutched at the air.

An ignominious end perhaps for one such as she. Yet strangely appropriate—as endings always are. Ursula was not offended by the highchair. And she rather liked the nursing home staff. They were, for the most part, friends of children. No, it was not the situation in which she found herself that generated fear. It was the terrible realization that she must take this final step alone.

Mighty Gretchen, fierce protector of all children,
Intercede for us.
Helpless and terrified—
Irreplaceable individuality returns to dust.
Solitary, corporate, all-being in ourselves,
We await the final demand.
Guardian hawk,
Rekindle our hearts within us.
Children of the morning, crying out for love—
They must grow and we must disappear.
Awesome messenger,
Be present with us at the hour of death.

Outside in the night, like some phantom creature from another world, the hawk traveled resolutely toward the place where Ursula had been taken. Ever faster she flew, her screams shattering the darkness.

Hatfield

I

"Of course you realize he has dhariki powers," said one of the translucent creatures who had been summoned.

"As a matter of principle he will not use dhariki," Tolak replied. His words had a hollow sound.

"A man of principle," the second creature laughed.

Tolak stared at them. "Jennings says stop him at all costs. Do you understand?"

Nefid and Droh understood. Nevertheless, any thought of confronting Hatfield was profoundly disturbing.

"Where is he?" asked Droh.

"In the forest at present. Traveling southwest. He is searching for the wolf's lair."

"How do you suggest we stop him?" Nefid said uneasily.

"In the name of Hell," hissed Tolak. "I don't know. Tell him you have word from the wolf. Threaten him with death. Just get the job done."

Nefid and Droh looked at each other, then at Tolak. Neither of them spoke.

"Hatfield must be stopped," Tolak went on. "Jennings will not tolerate failure in this matter."

II

Quite unaware of these developments, Hatfield moved swiftly along his way. The narrow sheath affixed to his left forearm held a thin blade of tempered steel— its handle resting just above the wrist. In addition, he carried a heavy wooden staff. And a wineskin filled with water was slung over one shoulder.

After a while he arrived at a clearing near the forest's edge. Hatfield was about to cross when he sensed a presence in that place. Something or someone was there. The traveler stopped and raised his staff.

"Who are you?" Hatfield called out.

"Messengers," Droh said, his voice faltering.

"We bring word from the wolf," Nefid added quickly.

"So . . . messengers." Hatfield did not move. "What word do you bring?"

"Wrong path," Nefid replied. "You are traveling southwest. Wolf is due east."

Hatfield let this thought spread across his mind. The wolf sends directions to his lair? Unlikely.

"Due east," Nefid said again with conviction.

Hatfield appeared to be considering the matter. "Journey to the East, is it?"

"Exactly," Nefid agreed.

"What else does the wolf want me to know?"

Droh could not resist answering. "He has prepared a feast for you. A reward for the work you have accomplished."

The traveler shook his head in bewilderment. Not only does the wolf send directions to his lair, but now he offers a reward. Without question, these two were impostors. Hatfield grasped the staff with both hands. His voice was barely audible.

"The wolf did not send you. Your words are those of Jennings. Stand aside or I'll flatten both of you."

"Damn you, Hatfield!" Nefid exclaimed. "Turn back or die!"

"You are prepared to kill me?"

"We are."

"Minion! Fool! You threaten Hatfield with death?"

"We know of your dhariki powers," said Droh. "We also know that you will not use them."

Hatfield looked surprised. "Is that what Jennings told you?"

"Jennings himself did not send us," Nefid replied. "We work for Tolak."

"Then it was Tolak who said I would not use dhariki?"

"Yes."

"And you believed him?"

"Why not?"

Hatfield shrugged. "Because Tolak is a liar. I will use dhariki."

Nefid did not wait. He screamed, jerked his sword from its scabbard and ran toward Hatfield swinging the weapon wildly.

Then when he was within five feet of his opponent, the translucent creature suddenly dropped low to the ground and spun about twice with astonishing skill. The blade made a whistling sound as it cut through the air where Hatfield's legs should have been.

Simultaneously, Droh removed an irregular metallic disc from his belt pouch. Raising his hand to hurl the object, he realized Hatfield was gone.

Nefid and Droh moved around the clearing—their eyes searching for some sign of the traveler.

"He's disappeared," Droh whispered.

"Dhariki!" Nefid's dread was palpable. "Hatfield is still in the clearing. Be careful."

With his sword, Nefid repeatedly and systematically slashed each quadrant of the space surrounding him.

"He's not here," Droh said again.

Exasperated, Nefid turned to reprimand his companion. What he saw was Droh lying face up on the ground. Near his right hand lay the irregular metallic disc.

"*Hatfield!*" Nefid yelled.

"You should never have believed Tolak." Hatfield's voice spoke from behind. Nefid felt something sharp strike hard just beneath his left shoulder blade. Before he could speak, he went unconscious.

"Tolak. . . ." Hatfield mused as he continued to make his way along the southwest passage leading out of the forest. "No, it isn't over. Jennings will not let matters rest here." He moved quickly, tapping with his staff, listening, now and again turning his head to better hear the sounds around him. Hatfield was a dhariki master. But he was also blind.

III

Jennings spoke from a remote sector of region five. "Hatfield was to have been stopped."

"Nefid and Droh were dispatched," Tolak said.

"They have failed."

"I do not understand. . . ."

"You *do* understand, sir. They were inadequately prepared. You told them Hatfield would not use dhariki."

"I thought it best."

"You didn't think at all, Tolak," Jennings said evenly. "Hatfield has passed through the Nindra Forest and is even now on his way to the Desert of Tabib. You are relieved of any further responsibility in this matter. I myself shall be waiting for Hatfield when he reaches Tabib."

IV

Desert's edge—Hatfield sensed the vast wasteland before him. Sand was warm to the touch. Air was cool, almost chilling. The traveler concluded he had arrived at this place just after dark. Hatfield sat down to rest.

He reflected: Best to keep going and cross by night. But can the journey be accomplished before daybreak? To be in the middle of the desert when the sun comes up, even with water and provisions, means death. I must cross at night—tonight, tomorrow night, it's all the same. But how far to the other side? There's no way to be certain. The wolf demands a journey and gives no directions. He never offers answers. The result is incalculable risk on an unknown desert—headed in a direction one can only guess at.

Hatfield was confounded. His own thoughts stopped him like a wall. In truth, he could not be sure of anything.

The blind man continued to sit motionless at the desert's edge. Then from a place somewhere deep within him, another idea broke through: Jennings. How subtle. How characteristic. To use my own mind to defeat me. Rational arguments designed to kill the spirit.

"Very clever, Jennings," Hatfield said aloud. "Master of 'what if' and 'first be sure of the way.' Purveyor of a truth that brings about inaction." But then immediately the traveler speculated: What if it's not Jennings? What if I am simply facing facts?

"Incredible," Hatfield laughed. "I'm at it again. No. It's Jennings all right. Far greater than Tolak."

Without hesitating, Hatfield scrambled to his feet and stepped forth into the desert. Repeatedly swinging his staff in a wide arc, he moved silently through the cold night air. A breeze cut across his body from left front to right rear. Hatfield kept moving—traveling blind, trusting the wind.

After what seemed like several hours, it occurred to Hatfield that the wind might have shifted without his perceiving it. In spite of these doubts, however, he kept on his way—remembering the cunning methods of Jennings.

To his surprise there was no noise when the staff

suddenly connected with something ahead of him. Hat-field stopped short. Once again he swung the staff in a wide arc. A jarring sensation like that of hitting a tree. But there was no sound.

"Mr. Hatfield, you are a stubborn man."

"Jennings?"

"Quite so, sir."

"Here in person?"

"Does that surprise you, Hatfield?"

"I suppose not. . . ."

"I shouldn't have thought so. Come now, shall we get straight to the point? You must abandon this jour-ney, if for no other reason than that you are no longer able to continue. Dhariki is of no avail. And you cannot get around me. As I am certain you are aware, Mr. Hatfield, I am *real*—unlike Tolak and his people."

"I know you are real," Hatfield acknowledged.

"And far more powerful than you."

"Agreed."

"Well then?"

"I'm thinking," responded the blind dhariki master.

"May I remind you that what you are attempting is impossible? No one can search out the wolf's lair."

"Yes. I know that."

"Then your journey is futile in any event."

"If the journey were *utterly* futile, Jennings, you would not be so determined to stop me."

"But that brings us back to the beginning, Mr. Hatfield. If I am, as you say, determined to stop you . . . how do you propose to continue?"

"I'm thinking."

"It's not too late to turn back," Jennings said without emotion.

Hatfield's mind raced. Jennings was telling the truth when he said no one could search out the wolf's lair. But it didn't follow that the wolf could not be found. If the whole journey were meaningless, why would Jennings interfere? Why involve Tolak? Hatfield was sure that the wolf could be found—not by searching, not by waiting. The journey itself was of utmost importance. From the first, Hatfield had believed he was on the right track. Now Jennings' reaction confirmed it. *Not by searching. Not by waiting.* He would never find the wolf. The wolf would find him.

"What do you think, Hatfield? Is it not wiser to abandon the project?"

The blind man moved suddenly, somersaulting forward. In the next instant he had slammed the staff upward with full force. The blow would have been fatal to another opponent. Under the present circumstances, however, Hatfield had a sense of having just attacked infinite mass and weight. The heavy wooden staff snapped in two like a twig.

"Stop it, Hatfield!" Jennings roared. "Your skill is not equal to the task."

The dhariki master circled slowly. "My skill is not equal to any of this, Jennings. So why not fight you?"

Hatfield jabbed with half of the broken staff. Then Jennings hit him. The traveler was knocked to the ground hard, but immediately regained his footing. Again Jennings lashed out. This time Hatfield grabbed instinctively and got hold of what felt like a tentacle—certainly not an arm. Quickly the thing wrapped itself around his neck. A second appendage lashed around his legs. Hatfield could not breathe. With his right hand he slapped at his left wrist. From its narrow sheath on his forearm, he managed to remove the thin blade of tempered steel. Without hesitating, Hatfield cut deep into the tentacle that was strangling him. Jennings bellowed and the blind man could feel an oily liquid oozing from the wound.

Now Hatfield could breathe. Immediately, however, he felt himself being lifted from the ground. Jennings continued to roar and bellow.

"Your power is limited," Hatfield gasped as Jennings raised him higher and higher above the desert. "You mobilized Tolak—the artful illusionist. *But the wolf sent you.* Oh, you are *real* enough, Jennings. Nevertheless, your power is limited. The wolf is ultimately responsible for what happens here." Hatfield had the sensation of spinning. Then the dhariki master was hurled onto the desert with such force that he lost consciousness.

V

"Enough, Jennings," the wolf said. "Here in the Desert of Tabib, it is I who have an appointment with Hatfield, not you."

"He is clever and ruthless," Jennings muttered.

"He is blind and unconscious," replied the wolf. "Leave him alone. Go now. Your work here is finished."

Without another word Jennings disappeared into darkness. The silver wolf stood for a moment looking at the traveler, who was barely breathing.

"You have astonishing courage, dhariki master," he said. "We have a great deal to talk about. And more to accomplish. But do not try to speak now. First you must rest from your journey."

Then like some fierce shepherd keeping watch by night, the great animal crouched beside Hatfield and growled at the desert surrounding them.

GUNFIGHTER

Words and Music by
Martin Bell

fore. He's an out-law— on the run, and he's

rid-ing— with the wind. And the last time——— I

saw him — it was out near— A-bi-lene. He's the

one they call the Gun-fight-er.

GUNFIGHTER

1. I dreamed last night I died and went to Houston.
   Met up with a solitary man.
   He wore his gun so low—I couldn't help but notice.
   And he carried a Bible in his hand.

   I saw he had spurs all made of silver.
   When he walked, he never made a sound.
   I thought it just as wise not to look into
        his eyes,
   So I kept on staring at the ground.

   > *Oh, I recognized him from before.*
   > *He's an outlaw on the run,*
   > *And he's riding with the wind.*
   > *And the last time I saw him—*
   > *It was out near Abilene.*
   > *He's the one they call the Gunfighter.*

2. In my dream I walked up to the stranger.
   Asked him if he didn't have a light.
   Then from his canteen, he poured water pure
        and clean,
   Saying, "Son, you'll be needing this tonight."

   Drank some of the water that he offered.
   You know I could swear that it was wine.

Then from the midnight darkness came the
    screaming of a demon,
And the stranger he cleared leather just in
    time.

> *Oh, I recognized him from before.*
> *He's an outlaw on the run,*
> *And he's riding with the wind.*
> *And the last time I saw him—*
> *It was out near Abilene.*
> *He's the one they call the Gunfighter.*

3. Shots rang out like thunder in the darkness.
   "Oh, my God," I cried. "Now there'll be hell
    to pay."
   The stranger he said, "Son, your journey's just
    begun.
   All along the way, the demons will be waiting."

Even then it seemed I must be dreaming.
The stranger he just left without a word.
I woke up last night and realized again
The danger of riding with the wind.

> *Oh, I recognized him from before.*
> *He's an outlaw on the run,*
> *And he's riding with the wind.*
> *And the last time I saw him—*
> *It was out near Abilene.*
> *He's the one they call the Gunfighter.*

Emmanuel

At a place not far from Golgotha
Certain shepherds kept watch by night.
Expecting just about anything but what happened.
Nonrational intrusion of unearthly purpose
Brought forth amidst earth-shattering holy screams.
There was nothing tender or mild about incarnation.
What happened was that Truth took shape.
And as a result of this unique illumination,
 the tables were turned on time and space.
Objects and actions and words and places—
 all participated in divine metamorphosis.
Therefore was he called Emmanuel. God with us.
Forsaken nomad, caught in a net of separation.
Crushed by historical necessity.
Yet the world's power did not prevail.
God had the final say
As shepherds kept watch by night.
 And this shall be a sign unto you; you shall
 not find the crucified one wrapped in the
 linens of death, nor lying in the tomb of
 Arimathea. He is alive; and he will be with
 you even unto the ends of the earth.
He is alive.
Encroaching now on earthly limits.
Fracturing sin and death and hell.

Flame within flame seeks out the hidden core.
Therefore is he called Emmanuel. God with us.
The captive, the poor, the blind, the oppressed,
      the lame—
Lifted up with him in glory.
The earth is the Lord's and the fullness thereof.
Blessed is he who yet becomes body and blood.
In a gaunt and barren land, creation unfolding still.
Eternity's countenance breaking through.
The first and the last. The root and the offspring
      of David.
Only God could be so human.
A bright morning star enlivens the sky.
Let those who are thirsty draw near.

> But men cannot look on the light when it's
> bright in the skies, when the wind has passed
> and cleared them. Out of Bethlehem's man-
> ger comes the Resurrected One; God all
> clothed in terrible majesty.

He shall come again with glory.
Saints and martyrs and prophets proclaim the new
      order.
Lift up your heads, O gates!
And be lifted up, O ancient doors!
Out of his heart shall flow rivers of living water.
And no one who drinks there will ever be thirsty
      again.
From a banquet of reconciliation does God return.
Toward an empty tomb and a manger bed is he
      traveling even now.
Nations will advance to his light, and kings to
      the brightness of his rising.

The Day of the Lord is upon us, every one.
Hosanna in the highest!
Behold a judge is standing at the door.
Therefore shall he be called Emmanuel. God with us.
The Mystery returning and claiming creation.
Blessed is he who comes to take us home.

Not Getting
Any Easier

"Come to bed," she murmured. "You've been up all night." Hers was a face unbetrayed by time. Parker lighted a cigarette and stared at the eastern sky.

"I'm somebody else now," he said. "The umbilical cord to my past has been severed. Dear Lorraine, how will you ever recognize me?"

"Parker," Lorraine said sleepily, hair spilling over her shoulders. "You're not somebody else. Nothing has changed."

"Nonsense, darling. The whole thing has been twisted out of shape. No longer are we experiencing anything like familiar surroundings. The environment has shifted utterly. And I am devoid of an organizing principle, or universe, by which to understand the situation."

"What on earth are you talking about?"

"Historical unrepeatability, untried juxtapositions of events and participants, new wine in old wineskins—that sort of thing."

"Oh, Parker." Lorraine touched his shoulder. "I swear, you get yourself into these predicaments by thinking too much."

Parker crushed out his cigarette. Then he stood

up, stretched, and walked over to the window. "But *without* thinking, we become victims of codified imaging. We view tomorrow merely as an extension of today. Contradictions disappear and the world seems to be frozen in place. Meanwhile, the future is tumbling over us like a raging river."

"I know," Lorraine said gently. "I know. It's just that I'm terribly concerned for you. You can't sleep, you're depressed—"

"My depression is part of it, I suppose. It's discouraging to be searching for your own shadow in the midst of cataclysmic world transition. But apply this kind of stress to humans, and what can you expect? Jobs have disappeared. The global economy is collapsing. We are teetering on the brink of nuclear holocaust. And systematically, irreversibly, the earth's atmosphere is being destroyed."

"I'm *worried* about you, that's all."

"Worried, yes. . . ." Parker watched as dark skies welcomed the first rays of sun. Then he reached in his bathrobe pocket for cigarettes, remembered they were on the coffee table and turned from the window to retrieve them.

He's aged so, Lorraine thought.

"The mind behaves erratically when it's overloaded," Parker continued. "Fatigue, confusion, and nervous irritability are correlates of today's experience."

"At least you could see a doctor. I don't think you're dealing with a simple matter here."

"I couldn't agree more, Lorraine. But sadly, we

are caught in an economic vise. There is virtually no money left and our health insurance has been cancelled for nonpayment. We're up against it, so to speak."

"Doctor Williamson would see you regardless."

"Perhaps. But then what? How am I to be treated for chronic alienation brought on by the breakdown of linear time?"

"Parker, please don't be ironic. It frightens me."

"Darling, I wasn't being ironic. At present I am facing options so unfamiliar, so untested, that neither past experience nor inherited wisdom offers the slightest assistance. It's not simply a matter of finding a job in a time of high unemployment. The point is that the jobs for which I am qualified don't exist any more. Over half of what is now available hadn't even been conceived when we were being educated."

Early morning light revealed a sparely-furnished flat. Of peculiar interest were certain decorations which had been carefully arranged on the kitchen table. Lorraine noticed them, and immediately the sting of tears caused her to turn away. "You've . . . put out the Christmas things," she said.

"Life was full of exciting and wonderful chances once, wasn't it, Lorraine?" Parker sat on the couch absently holding an unlighted cigarette.

Lorraine could not look at him. She kept thinking about how he had been awake all night worrying—and preparing for Christmas. The loneliness, the loss of structure, the collapse of meaning in his life obviously went only so far. At his center, Parker was possessed of a hidden spiritual tenacity. In spite of this, however, Lorraine honestly wondered how much more stress he could withstand.

"When I was growing up, I used to have a little stuffed bear," Parker said as if the thought followed naturally. "Years went by. Then one day I couldn't find it. I never knew what happened to the animal—only that it was gone. I believe my childhood must have ended the day I couldn't find that bear."

"Oh, Parker, I'm losing *you*, not some stuffed animal. I mean you can't just drift away from me one day. Do you hear what I'm saying? I won't have it!" Lorraine sat down on the vacant end of the couch and bridged her fingers over her eyes.

There was a short silence. Then Parker said, "Do you want breakfast? I think there's some orange juice in the refrigerator. And we have enough money to get bagels . . . that is, if you want breakfast."

His voice trailed off, and Lorraine didn't even try to answer. She bit hard at her lower lip, then finally allowed her body to convulse with sobbing. Half asleep now, Parker muttered, "Don't cry, darling. . . ." But exhaustion overtook him before the thought was complete.

"You leave him alone," Lorraine said aloud to the room. "You let him have Christmas without scaring him like this, understand? Just leave him alone!" So saying, she choked on her tears and sank to the floor. There, part crouching, part kneeling, she rocked back and forth in silent protest.

As a matter of fact, they had no orange juice. A

small detail, maybe. But Lorraine found herself obsessed by the idea that at least she could remedy this. With an almost missional attitude, she began heating pans of water on the stove and carrying them to the bathroom. She adjusted the temperature of her tub by adding cold water from the faucet, bathed quickly, and got dressed.

Next she took a little box of money out from underneath the dresser and dumped its contents onto the bed. Lorraine counted fifty-three dollars seventy-six cents, pocketed a twenty-dollar bill, and replaced the rest. Without hesitating, she grabbed the overcoat with the sort of fur collar, and pulled it on. Then she placed a note for Parker on the coffee table beside him, gently brushed back some hair from his forehead, and left the apartment.

Once outside, Lorraine walked three blocks to a delicatessen where, with no outward display of emotion, she purchased fresh orange juice and some bagels. She felt the expected sense of accomplishment. But there was also an unaccountable aching deep within her bones when she stepped forth from the shop with these sacraments.

A disjointed and apparently unreal time it was in their life together. More stunned than oblivious to the season, Lorraine made her way along Christmas streets. And so it happened that, returning, she came upon a variety store and stopped for a moment to gaze in the window. Prominently displayed among multiple inexpensive offerings sat a tiny stuffed bear. Lorraine hesitated for a long while before going inside.

"How much for that little bear?" she asked, pointing at the display.

The shopkeeper did not look up from the magazine he was reading. "Eight ninety-five plus tax, and you take it home for under the tree."

"Done," replied Lorraine.

"Gift wrapped is extra," said the man, still reading.

"Not necessary," Lorraine said. "I'll take it as is." Then she produced ten dollars and the shopkeeper got the stuffed animal for her.

"Need a bag?"

"No thank you . . . just the bear." Lorraine tucked the animal inside her coat, waited for change, and hurriedly left the store.

It was nearly noon. Now she could hear the sound of Christmas music punctuated by traffic noises, and in the distance, a siren. For an instant, Lorraine lost track of where she was, but she kept on walking anyway—one hand holding the sack of groceries, the other tightly hugging the bear beneath her coat.

At the next corner, she managed to regain a sense of location and time reference. The city looked familiar again. Headed in her direction from across the street came a laughing young couple, arms full of holiday packages. She stood absolutely still and watched their approach, while memories of other Christmases welled up inside. Then as the young strangers were about to pass by, Lorraine suddenly stepped in front of them. "He's going to make it," she said. "You'll see."

PROMISES

Words and Music by
Martin Bell

CHORUS

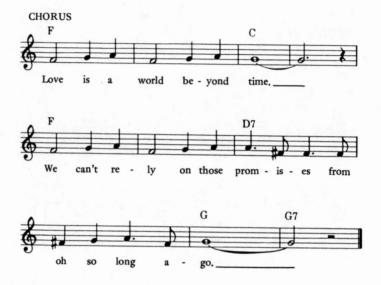

Love is a world be - yond time. _____

We can't re - ly on those prom - is - es from

oh so long a - go. _____

PROMISES

1. Promises, they never last.
   Stay with me here tonight.
   And let your love
   Restore my soul again.

   Beauty fades, as it surely must,
   But those who love cannot forget.
   And I'll not let you go
   When falling leaves come down.

   > *Love is a world beyond time.*
   > *We can't rely on those promises*
   > *From oh so long ago.*

2. Shadows, they give way to light,
   Stay with me here tonight.
   I've seen too much,
   And, Lord, I'm not that strong.

   Don't say the words. I know you've changed.
   But those who love have no regrets.
   Please don't explain
   What we both understand.

   > *Love is a world beyond time.*
   > *We can't rely on those promises*
   > *From oh so long ago.*

Broken Through Now

I

"She's broken through by now," he said.
"I somehow fell behind."
He stood surrounded by the dead,
As cold November wind
Brought to his aged, grieving head
New clarity of mind.

It was by passion's wild excess
That love for them was spurred.
So when at last the pain ingressed,
She held him with her words.
In whispering did she caress,
More to be felt than heard.

A few leaves clinging desperately
Recalled for him again
The moments of despondency—
The times when it had been
Unbearable to watch, to see
That struggle at the end.

O frightful, bleak November dawn!
Never to be the same,

Enrapt with glory on this lawn,
Back from the dead he came.
And walked out from the tombs as one
Who nurtured holy flame.

II

He chose a place near Framingham
To spend his final years.
There no one sought to understand
When laughter mixed with tears
Came rushing through the bursted dam
Of memories and fears.

Caught in a world he never made,
A labyrinth of doubt,
He lived in hope. He learned to pray.
Then seven years without
Her changed hope to bitter waiting,
The prayers to angry shouts.

His heart, his soul cried out for more.
The enemy was death.
And now for spite did he endure.
But carefully beneath
A rigid countenance was stored
The final emptiness.

Dark despair the reverse of hope
Is not. It's apathy

That envelops the soul with loathsome
Nothing and ratcheting
Void. He fought this interloper
From beyond. And lost.

III

A boundless, barren twilight realm
Swallowed him up alive.
He saw himself as unredeemed,
An empty thing deprived
Of human passion. Overwhelmed
And hollowed out inside.

Then through the streets of Framingham,
Wrapped in a tattered shawl,
A shadow figure made its way
To where he lay enthralled
By lethargy. In this gray place
She hovered near the wall.

The assessment of the townsfolk
Was that he had died alone.
They wagged their heads and sadly spoke
Of how withdrawn he'd been.
Never to love was his mistake,
They said. Then buried him.

"Wake up, you old man," was the call
He had heard. Spirited

Shouts and laughing embraces all
Followed. She said,
"You've broken through!" And they fell
Into clouds together.

Midway of
the Jackals

Somewhere on a beach near a great expanse of water there are brightly-colored canvas pavilions, wooden booths constructed without thought to permanence, and a variety of smaller tents painted with vertical stripes. In that place a carnival atmosphere prevails. It is the home of Chudan-ko, the pirate. However, over a span of years, it has also become a haven for lonely, frightened outcasts—a sanctuary for creatures who have no place else to go.

Gently rising and falling on the sea, its wooden masts creaking and swaying, the pirate's ship is anchored nearby. At first glance there appears to be a striking contrast between this battered old vessel and the marvelous hullabaloo on shore.

Chudan-ko is seated outside his tent talking with Ramone. In the distance one hears a calliope sound mixed with clamorous voices of dogged pitchmen hawking their wares. Banners of every description have been unfurled throughout the area.

"Enormous cat," Ramone says, observing a large animal headed toward them.

"That's a leopard," Chudan-ko replies. "But don't

be concerned. You are my guest and a visitor in this place. The leopard will not harm you."

Ramone accepts the word of assurance while continuing to stare uneasily in the cat's direction. "What a fascinating experience," he remarks.

An ancient woman cries out, "Bear witness to me, Chudan-ko. For my husband, he was wrested from me in his thirty-seventh year."

The leopard snarls and the old one steps back quickly.

"Walk on by, woman," the pirate shouts. "Yet again I bear witness to your complaint. And once more shall I say that life is worth the dying."

"She seems greatly distressed," Ramone comments.

"Her husband died many years ago," says Chudan-ko, slowly standing up. "Every day she comes here. It is always the same. She yells at me and I yell back. The woman has lived for nearly a century. More than half these years have been spent on the midway."

"The midway?"

"Come, my friend," Chudan-ko answers. "Let us walk together along the Midway of the Jackals. You will understand more after we have been there." The pirate takes up a crossbow and fits an arrow into it. Then, holding the weapon loosely in his left hand, he throws his right arm around Ramone's shoulders.

As they start off, a hunchback appears and blocks the way. He addresses Ramone without actually looking at him. "Enough is enough, child. And too much is not enough. Beware the Midway of the Jackals lest you find that it is too much."

"Why does he speak thus to me?" the visitor exclaims.

Chudan-ko waves the hunchback aside and they continue. But Ramone is not at all sure he likes the answer given by his host. "The man has divine insight. Be sure to pay him heed. What he says could save your life."

"You make it sound dangerous."

"There is always danger," Chudan-ko smiles. "Especially on the midway. That is why the leopard travels with us."

Ramone does not immediately see the cat. He looks ahead and to either side.

"Behind you," the pirate explains without breaking stride.

The visitor does not look back. It is bad enough to have a leopard at your heels, he thinks.

Soon there is activity everywhere: jugglers and clowns, a hall of mirrors, a dancing bear, and acrobats. There are various sideshows and concession stands with barkers all competing to be heard over the noise of the crowd. A calliope has been placed so that its music provides a unifying strand for the whole chaotic scene.

Carrying an outlandish array of balloons, a midget walks straight toward the pirate and his companions. "Welcome to the midway, Chudan-ko," the grinning vendor says while hopping, quite deliberately, first on one foot then the other. "Assorted shapes and colors today. Balloons of every kind. Best buy on the midway, my balloons. Two for a penny. Assorted colors and shapes for a limited time only. Hurry, hurry, hurry."

"We'll take two," Chudan-ko announces. "One for me and one for my guest." He produces a penny, and the midget hands a balloon to each of them.

"What about the leopard?" Ramone whispers.

"He doesn't want a balloon," says Chudan-ko as they begin to walk along the Midway of the Jackals.

Near one of the concession booths, Ramone sees a distinguished-looking man wearing a sandwich board. Apart from the placard hanging over his shoulders, he looks like a prosperous executive—impeccably groomed and attired in a charcoal-gray business suit. An odd juxtaposition, Ramone thinks, his eyes fixed on the sandwich board's message: *No Time Left.*

In an alcove across the way, there is a table draped with burlap and silk. An attractive young woman is seated there studying tarot cards. As Ramone approaches, she calls out, "Learn what the future holds. Visit Sylvia before you continue on. Personal readings are absolutely without charge." Behind the fortune teller's table is a panel bearing the words: *Every Answer Questioned.*

Ramone turns to the pirate. "Whatever does this mean?" he asks. Chudan-ko, however, is not paying attention. He is enthralled by the fat lady seated on a platform high above the crowd. Next to her stands a somber little boy pointing to a hand-lettered sign that reads: *Necessary and Received.* From time to time, the fat lady proclaims with some secret authority, "All in free. All in free." Whenever she says this, the little boy nods vigorously and applauds. To Ramone's surprise, his host responds similarly.

"Listen to her, Ramone! She is announcing the final word about life in history. The fat lady is speaking to everything and everyone—past, present, and future." Chudan-ko continues to applaud each time he hears the woman speak.

An unshaven, wild-eyed man staggers by. "Burn in hell, worthless pirate," he shouts. "You are no better than the fools that line the midway."

"We all belong here, Nandor," Chudan-ko declares. "Stop accusing the you in me. There is no quarrel between us."

"Wait a minute," Ramone interrupts. "There is too much going on. My mind cannot encompass it."

Both Nandor and Chudan-ko look at Ramone. And the leopard moves closer. "Perhaps the young visitor has had enough?" suggests Nandor.

"Too much is not enough," Chudan-ko reminds the wild-eyed one. "My friend here speaks of *too much*. Give him a chance. I trust he is remembering what the hunchback said."

"He has already decided against us," Nandor laughs. "And who could blame him? We are, after all, nothing more than a conglomeration of hermits and jackals and thieves."

Decided against us? Ramone wonders why Nandor would think that. "On this midway, everything and everyone is necessary and received," he hears himself saying.

Nandor is strangely disconcerted by these words. Without speaking, he turns and walks away. For one who had staggered earlier, he now moves with surprising agility and ease.

"Utterly amazing," Ramone says to the pirate. "However did you find this place?"

"I didn't," Chudan-ko responds. "One day I just showed up on shore. Apparently there was a reason for my arriving here. Or at least I believed such to be the case."

Ramone looks again at the busy midway. "Was the beach like this when you found it?"

"Not actually. The area was more desolate in those days. Lonely and frightened people would seek it out from time to time. But they wouldn't stay long. The tents, the calliope, and the concession booths were my idea. Added a touch of color, I thought. In any event, I made my home here, and slowly the others began to join me. Together we created the midway and everything else that you see." After speaking, Chudan-ko stands motionless, holding a festive balloon in one hand and a deadly crossbow in the other.

There is something very right about all that I have seen, Ramone thinks. Then, without really knowing why, he says, "I was mistaken, Chudan-ko. It is not too much for me. It is, I believe, exactly enough."

"Almost certainly you are the one I have expected," the pirate replies. "*Too much* is for those who have time. *Enough* is more to the point when there is no time left. Come, my friend, we must return to our tents without delay."

Now the leopard takes the lead as they move through the crowd. There is still a good deal of jostling and shouting going on, but Ramone is no longer aware of his surroundings. Over and over again he ponders Chudan-ko's words: Almost certainly you are the one I have expected.

Once they are back at the tents, Chudan-ko replaces the crossbow on its rack and ties the two balloons nearby. After sitting down, he smiles in Ramone's direction. The visitor remains standing. Chudan-ko allows his gaze to travel out over the shimmering expanse of water before him. "What do you know of your own arrival here, Ramone?"

"Curiously, it would seem that I got to this shore in much the same way you did. One day, without warning, I just showed up on the beach."

"You have no idea why or how?"

"None."

The pirate continues to watch evening sunlight dance on the sea. "I rather suspected you might be my successor," he says calmly.

Ramone hesitates before speaking. Yet the idea of being Chudan-ko's successor does not seem in the least strange to him. "How will I ever manage that?" he asks, without questioning the pirate's insight.

"Take everything as it comes, Ramone. Don't plan ahead or attempt to design a strategy. As you have seen, life on the midway brings many surprises. One may not rely on accumulated knowledge or past experience."

"But what will happen to you, Chudan-ko? Some-

thing in your words makes my spirit grow uneasy.
Perhaps I am afraid that you are going to die."

"On the contrary, my friend. Apparently there is
another task to be accomplished. We must not reason it
out, however, lest the reasoning give rise to particular
expectations."

"Every answer questioned?" Ramone suggests.

"I shall return to the midway alone tonight," the
pirate goes on, almost as if his companion had not
spoken. "The leopard will stay with you."

Upon uttering these words, he stands up and places
both hands on the younger man's shoulders. For the
next moment Chudan-ko looks hard into Ramone's
eyes. Then he says again, "The leopard will stay with
you."

It is an uncanny experience to see Chudan-ko
walking by himself back along the path to the midway.
Noticing the pirate's weapon still mounted on its rack,
Ramone thinks: He has forgotten the crossbow.

After supper, the young man wraps a cloak around
himself and sits on the beach awaiting Chudan-ko's
return. Several hours later he becomes restless and
wonders why the pirate is taking so long. He resolves to
wait up all night if necessary. But soon thereafter,
lulled by the sound of waves against the shore, Ramone
falls asleep.

Quietly they come now. Single file along the shore,
the pirate's crew approaches. Starlight and a bold half
moon illuminate the scene. First Chudan-ko, then Nan-
dor and the dancing bear appear. Sylvia the fortune
teller is followed by two acrobats, the balloon man, and
many others.

From where Ramone is sleeping, the leopard watches this raggedy band of creatures. They are searching in and around some tents near the water. Within minutes, several dinghies and multiple sets of oars have been retrieved from their hiding places.

The pirate motions with his hand and the others carry these small boats into the water. One vessel is steadied as the bear is helped inside. Next, everyone is climbing over gunwales. Oars are placed in oarlocks, and the dinghies glide silently toward Chudan-ko's battered frigate.

Once at the ship, a hasty boarding is effected. The smaller boats are hoisted up and fastened into place. Now it seems each member has some predetermined charge. Intently rigging sails and swabbing decks, the crew makes ready for departure.

Soon canvas billows out against a moonlit sky, and imperceptibly the ship is under way. The glorious craft moves dreamlike across an open sea, while back on shore the leopard waits for dawn.

Except for the sound of seagulls and pounding surf, the beach is silent when Ramone comes to life again. Encouraged by the sun's warm touch, he stretches for a moment before sitting up. Then, half awake, he stares at the leopard and realizes what must have happened.

"Good Lord, I fell asleep," he says aloud.

At once the young man stands up and casts his cloak aside. Apparently Chudan-ko did not return from the midway last night. But there's more to it than that. Something very basic has changed. Methodically he studies the surrounding area. Pavilions, tents, and ban-

ners are all the same. The leopard has not moved.
Chudan-ko's crossbow is right where he left it. Apart
from the silence, Ramone cannot immediately find a
source for his uneasiness. Then absently he gazes at the
great expanse of water where yesterday a ship was
resting at anchor. What he sees, or rather doesn't see,
causes the young man to draw in his breath.

Overcome by a sudden feeling of helplessness,
Ramone tries desperately to fit the pieces together.
Has the pirate simply taken everyone away, leaving
him and the leopard stranded on this shore? The con-
clusion is not unthinkable.

"Not unthinkable, perhaps," says a voice from
behind. "But mistaken nevertheless."

Ramone turns around without knowing what to
expect. There, all alone, is the somber little boy from
the midway. For a time, each regards the other with
suspicion. Then Ramone virtually shouts at the boy,
"Do you know what's going on here?"

As if this were a signal, the somber one raises both
arms above his head and intones, "Necessary and re-
ceived. Necessary and received." In the distance a
calliope begins to play, and clamor from the midway
provides counterpoint to the boy's chanting.

"Enough is enough," yells the hunchback, who
appears for a moment, then is gone.

And before Ramone can judge, analyze or decide
what any of this means, he is challenged by an ancient
woman's cry, "Bear witness to me, Ramone. For my
husband, he was wrested from me in his thirty-seventh
year."

OUT OF CONTROL

Words and Music by
Martin Bell

Ev-'ry-bod-y knows that grow-ing up is nev-er eas-y.

It's a price you have to pay no mat-ter

how much you don't want to. And the time will come—

when you fi - nal - ly de-cide—

Yes-ter-day is gone a-way and nev-er com-ing back here.

But the world of make-be-lieve is still a

place you like to turn to. While the ca - rou - sel ___

keeps on spin - ning round and round —

CHORUS

Out of con - trol. That's how it goes— spin - ning, or so it

seems. Life's bro-ken dreams_turn-ing a - round now._

OUT OF CONTROL

1. Everybody knows that growing up is never easy.
   It's a price you have to pay no matter how
         much you don't want to.
   And the time will come
   When you finally decide—

   Yesterday is gone away and never coming back
         here.
   But the world of make-believe is still a place
         you like to turn to.
   While the carousel
   Keeps on spinning round and round—

   Out of control.
   That's how it goes—spinning,
   Or so it seems.
   Life's broken dreams turning around now.

2. Well, you make a quick appearance as you're
         heading for the border.
   You can put it all behind your eyes and wait
         for repercussions.
   You've got the ring of truth.
   Yes, it's yours to use until you go and—

   Lay your money down and buy a ticket to the side-
         show.

And you wonder why you did it when you hadn't
    even planned to go.
Then you enter through the gate
And tell the ticket-taking lady that you're—

Out of control.
That's how it goes—spinning,
Or so it seems.
Life's broken dreams turning around now.

3. Yesterday is gone away and never coming back
        here.
   But the world of make-believe is still a place
        you like to turn to.
   While the carousel
   Keeps on spinning round and round—

Out of control.
That's how it goes—spinning,
Or so it seems.
Life's broken dreams turning around now.

Journal of Adrienne Hogarth

Occasional Reflections and Reminders of a Generally Theological Nature

Entry for April 21

Is it merely the tinted glass, or has the sun been swallowed by some unfriendly cloud? A single sapling, no taller than I am—stretching every fiber of its being to touch the sky—somehow gives me hope. We are not so different, I think.

The place whereon we stand is holy ground.

I feel driven forward into an unknown region. Am I seeking—or being sought?

Entry for April 22

I don't think anybody ever intended to be a prophet. It just isn't something a person would want to do. The whole business is untenable, undesirable, humanly impossible stuff. Not surprisingly, there seems to have been a certain reluctance—even recalcitrance—on the part of those elected. Moses said: Who am I that I should go to Pharaoh and bring the children of Israel out of Egypt? Jonah fled into Tarshish to escape the presence of the Lord. Ezekiel went in bitterness, in the heat of his spirit, the hand of the Lord being strong upon him.

Thrown up against kings, priests, political leaders—often the entire social order. Precipitated by unearthly outsight. The prophets were not called. They were driven.

Entry for April 23

Clearly, hope is not the same thing as knowledge or certitude. And that leaves a good deal of unknowing floating around.

Kierkegaard: An artist and a prophet—slow to use the word ghostly because it didn't apply to him for the most part. Also, he was somewhat shy when people asked about holy and transcendent things.

I'm beginning to believe the theological enterprise has something to do with a special journey—a long and difficult path upward from the waters of my birth. Great bushlands ablaze. Streams frozen over. Fierce animals stalking through tropical rain forests.

Why does it seem so important to remember that I used to go to sleep with the radio on just to know someone else was out there?

Entry for April 25

The prophets must have possessed an enhanced sense of identity with all people. For example, Isaiah wrote: Woe is me for I am a man of unclean lips and I live in the midst of a people of unclean lips.

Some were from the higher class; some came from the wilderness. Gloriously one-sided forth-tellers. They spoke of a height beyond reckoning. Fully immersed in history, they proclaimed the Divine Word.

Entry for April 26

Death, in a variety of disguises, has a way of inter-rupting—every time. It would be possible (even if inadvisable) to say that life is all about death. It sounds peculiar when you say it out loud. But the unspoken thought is rational enough. Besides, I'll warrant there has to be a great deal of power (?) in anything that can sneak up on us that successfully. And whether it is masked as hostility, despair, self-contempt, or finality—death is sneakier than anything in the world.

Entry for April 29

Went downtown today and by chance met Trish Mc-
Carthy. Found out she spent six months on a psychiat-
ric ward last year. She says she writes poetry every
morning.

Life is real wherever it is being lived. But, if appear-
ances are to be believed, it's more difficult for some
than for others.

Entry for June 2

What did Bill mean by "as things stand at present"?
Have we adopted a language concocted in the fun
house?

I sense a path leading up the side of the mountain—a
path that is headed somewhere. Irresistibly drawn to-
ward a spiritual destiny, I am becoming more solitary—
necessarily, I think. Yet in the midst of even the most
inward-focused moments—something always intrudes.
Why? Am I looking in the wrong place?

Entry for June 3

When our forebears prayed, it was not wishful thinking.

Entry for June 4

I may be onto something. It's hard to put it into words. But I'd rather try to express myself—even partially—than lose track of this.

Daily devotions, meditation, attending worship—these are helpful to the spiritual quest. But they can also get in the way.

Although it might be possible to transcend a given moment or way of thinking, it is not possible to transcend the human condition. No amount of spiritual striving will ever change my humanness, I suspect.

And when I feel set apart from other people (because of certain ideas or practices), my soul becomes stultified.

Entry for June 6

True spirituality is not a way of escaping human suffering—nor does it set up barriers separating individuals from each other.

Piety is not the same thing as pietism.

It's good for people to be exactly the way they are. Condemnation is easier than investigation.

Entry for June 7

The point is to become immersed in *reality*. Eyes to see, ears to hear. I've been searching selectively. There's so much more.

Jesus saw humanity with larger eyes. Our iniquity didn't take him off guard either. He was up to something too important for righteous indignation.

Monuments to God are not edifices we build, but moments of encounter—in the wildernesses of our own lives.

The blind newspaper vendor on the corner asked me a strange question today: How big is your dream?

Trish called and wouldn't talk very long. She sounded unhappy.

Entry for June 10

It seems to me that prayer usually begins on a selfish note.

Our forebears dared to call God to a reckoning. Jeremiah, for one, challenged God. Job cried out against the injustice visited on him. Moses demanded that God repent.

Bill said, "She's just one more nut case in a world of sad little people, Adrienne. A real nobody, going nowhere."

These days I find myself identifying with people I never even noticed before.

The stranger.
The prisoner.
The forgotten one.
Those who mourn
and those who can do nothing but despair.
Those who rejoice wildly
and those who are silent.

We are all children of the promise, riders of the storm— nameless, faceless ones who show forth unanticipated courage and who embody hope.

Maybe I have finally decided to be a person among persons. To endure, suffer, hope, celebrate, and die daily.

One time when Jesus was surrounded by many people, he suddenly asked, "Who touched me?" A murmur went through the crowd: Not me, not me. Peter pointed out the obvious—dozens of people were jostling the Master. Jesus asked again, "Who touched me?" One woman overcame her fear and confessed she had reached out and been healed. "Your faith has made you well. Go in peace," he said.

Beware of these illusions: I'm in control. I can perceive God's plan. I know what's ultimately good or evil.

Stop resisting—God goes in first place. (Not meditation, church, or the Bible.) Jeremiah reminds us that God is not nearly as interested in religion as we are.

Men and women of faith always trusted that God's purpose was being hammered out in the historical arena, regardless of who the players seemed to be or whatever evil appeared on stage.

In the face of what is, it would be easy to look away and relinquish the freedom to observe, to decide.

But on my journey to the mountain, I have discovered that God can transform brokenness, anxiety, and terror into wholeness.

Entry for June 13

After being healed, the Gadarene demoniac wanted to travel with the disciples. Jesus said no.

Once you get everything you want, you're going to find out *that* wasn't what you really wanted.

The Lone Ranger was pretty realistic. He sought to establish law and order more zealously than outlaws sought to disrupt it. What mask am I wearing? How big *is* my dream?

Entry for June 15

Joan of Arc: I never envied her at all. She lost control. She wouldn't eat. She counted her ribs (her inhalations too, no doubt), and her leather bag was empty, always empty.

I don't know why we tend to condemn the holy ones— the wild-eyed, half-crazy, sideways-walking holy ones.

It is a miracle that the words of the prophets were preserved at all. They were dissenters—speaking against governments and hollow rituals. They threatened every form of complacency and hypocrisy.

Passionately attached to God, historically grounded, despairing, but never apathetic. No magic. No foretelling. Just the searing Word. Thus saith the Lord! Repent! This day your life will be given back to you.

I asked the newspaper vendor, what about the blindness? Just the way it is, he said—tipping his red beret to invisible customers.

Entry for June 16

At 3:00 o'clock this morning, Patricia Eileen McCarthy took her own life.

Entry for June 30

Told Bill that the times have caught up with us, but we have not caught up with the times—God is mounting the pulpit and preaching his own sermon.

Bill said he would call me next week, but he didn't mean it.

I don't understand death any better today. Vast outpourings of love, great patience, and an abundance of honest humor may someday help me deal with *dying*. But I don't think I'll ever understand death. . . .

Entry for July 1

Top secret. Eyes only.

Spirituality is nothing more or less than putting God in first place. Responding to the still, small voice that demands—everything.

Entry for July 2

I can't stand it. It's too much for me. It's just too much.

Spirituality is the process by which a person is ripped apart.

Entry for September 7

Clearly, hope is not the same thing as knowledge or certitude.

Again I feel driven into an unknown region. Am I seeking—or being sought?

Stepping Out

[1] I'll tell you what (?)
  has happened—
  if words don't
give out.
That fierce-blade work of art
  just split
    my
    head
    apart.
  It's about time
      something
      cut through.
  I
have been
    dying
  inside (& outside too).
And (lonely) crying for
    a great
    experiencing.
  Now
    [Emphasis mine]
        finally—
        this (!)
  [Artistic turning from
      cold abyss;

The whole Jesus! urgency
      of life;
Wildwind
      catapulting
      silence(s);
Imaginative space]
                        crea-
                        ting love.

[2] That terrifying
                        music
                        of the fragile
            self
Conveys for me
      the one
                  test
                        of reality
Worth (radiant) bothering
                  with
                  at all.
So
play it, Joe!
                  Perform it,
            sing it,
                  bring it
                  on
Again (!) you'll
            find I'm
            ready
            (as I'll ever be)

To hear
  your
      song of
      life burst   forth—
[Structured arrange-
    ments falling
         in
         place;
Stabbing
    flashfire rhythms
          reaching out;
Words
      indwelt by
      furious-glowing
        grace
Ignite (!) and
    flare at last]
          into flame.

[3] Extraordinary
        feat of imagination:
Sound and fury (?)
    the outward and visible
        sign,
Healing (joyous)
          concealed
          therein.
Those long ago
  forgotten   (Break it
        open, Joe!)

Enchantments
                    beckon
                              to me.
                [Spotlight, center stage]
And I am   shaken
                         from the
                         dead—
[Earthquake
    searching God! for
             Chinatown;
Worldly clay
                              groaning and
                              cracking wide;
Layer
        upon
        crafted
        layer of
                    meaning;
Breathing
    sacred spirit]
                 of the night.

[4] What else is there
              to say (?)
          I knew
          when it happened
          You had managed to
                              lay hold
                              of the deep(est)
                              me.

Astonishing
          is the word for
This (night and day)
          journey.
                    It's your music (!)
playing
Havoc
          with my fatal
          neon-conformity.
[Exit stage right]
          I'm
          stepping
          out—
[Precarious way
          through the water-
                    fall;
Snowmelt
                    washing down
                    around the past;
Transcendent sound
     pushing beyond   and
Plummeting]
                    into another
                    world.

THE SWEEPER

Words and Music by
Martin Bell

They say___ he can't stay here no more.
Too man - y fam - 'lies to - geth - er. There's aunts and
un - cles and fa - thers and broth - ers and moth - ers and
sis - ters, just hop - ing to wake up to - mor - row. ___
___ Il - le - gal - ly liv - ing at eight;
where will he be when he's ten? ___ Ex -

THE SWEEPER

1. They say he can't stay here no more.
   Too many families together.
   There's aunts and uncles and fathers and
        brothers and mothers and sisters,
   Just hoping to wake up tomorrow.

   Illegally living at eight;
   Where will he be when he's ten?
   Exceeding the limits, I guess.
   Pitching pennies and sweeping the streets.

2. Laws are made to protect us.
   I know all about that and
   How it's not right when you crowd all those people—
        they start in on fighting and killing
   And mixing up loving with hating.

   But the light in my son's eyes is dying.
   And me, I've been working,
   So sick and afraid
   That they'll take him—and sweep him away.

   Refrain

3. This house, it ain't nothin' no more.
   It needs some shutters and painting

And gutters—we ain't got money to spend on
    the windows to keep out the cold.
And God knows how the roof's gonna hold.

But under the front porch you'll find
A place where a small boy
Can hide from the pain
Till the dreams come to sweep him away.

4. They say he can't stay here no more.
   The welfare department sends people
   To see us—writing their questions and answers
       on pre-printed tablets.
   They say that they know what they're doing.

But the man downtown never will see
How we laugh and we cry—
Exceeding the limits.
My son is sweeping the streets.

Refrain

They say he can't stay.

From New York
to Boston and Beyond

I

Once darkness fully settles in, there may come an emancipation of sorts, he thought. And why not? People pay a high enough price to arrive at this place. He was making faces in the mirror. A favorite was his God-but-I'm-fat look produced by lowering the chin until a significant skin roll appeared. If he pushed this loose skin back and forth with a thumb, the desired effect was achieved. He also liked creating what-if-I-had-a-facelift-and-it-didn't-work by pushing up hard on both cheeks with the bases of his palms until the eyes slanted and he couldn't breathe through his nose. At this very moment, however, he was enjoying my-health-is-failing-fast, a face best invoked when leaning toward the mirror as far as possible—pondering dark undereye circles, winter pallor, and thinning hair.

"Whatcha doing, Teddy?" asked a very small boy now standing in the bathroom doorway.

"Making faces," he said. "Need to get in here?"

"Mom says breakfast is on the table and you should come downstairs now."

My health *is* failing fast, Teddy thought, spending

a few more moments studying his closeup. "Tell her I'll be right there, Leonard."

"You gonna keep making faces for a while?"

"Yeah. . . ."

"Can I watch?"

"Well, it's O.K. by me if you watch. I mean, it really is fine by me. Only I thought you were going to tell your mother that I'm coming right down."

"Mom!" Leonard shouted, "Teddy's coming down as soon as—"

"For heaven's sake, Leonard!" Teddy said. "Don't yell like that, all right? I thought you were going down-stairs to tell her—"

"What's going on up there?" asked Mary Beth from the lower landing. "Teddy, is Leonard bothering you?"

"Driving me absolutely around the *bend!*" Teddy winked at the little boy. "Won't leave me alone while I'm making faces."

"What? I can't hear you, Teddy," Mary Beth said.

In sequence, Leonard stuck out his tongue, half-smiled, and ran from the doorway. Teddy could hear the child thumping and giggling all the way down the stairs. Eyes twinkling, he slapped on some cologne and straightened his tie. "Breakfast is served," he said rather formally. Then, as an afterthought, he stuck out his tongue at the old codger in the mirror before leaving the bathroom.

"Teddy—?" Mary Beth was halfway up the stairs.

"Never felt better," Teddy said, meeting her on

his way down. "Leonard mentioned something about breakfast's being on the table. And, wouldn't you know, there I was still getting ready."

"He said you were—"

"Making faces?"

"Teddy!"

"Well, that's exactly what I *was* doing, Mary Beth. He's right as rain on that score." Teddy took each step individually. "So what's for breakfast? Are you still able to get that fantastic marmalade from wherever it was you used to get it?"

"Grrr!" Leonard said, peeking around the dining room wall.

"You're utterly impossible, Teddy." Mary Beth laughed in spite of herself.

"Why? Because I like marmalade?" he said. "Lots of people like marmalade." Having reached the first floor, he headed straight for the dining room growler. "Grrr yourself, you little reprobate. I see you in there."

Delighted to have been found, Leonard squealed and escaped into the kitchen.

"Scrambled eggs, English muffins, and orange marmalade," Mary Beth said, indicating the linen-covered dining table. "How's that for remembering what you like? Oh, and coffee, of course—served after the meal."

Teddy nodded pleasantly and took a seat at the table. He made something of a project of opening his napkin to full width and tucking it under his chin. "Leonard," he said to the kitchen. "Your mother's humoring me with marmalade. What a dreadful thing to do to an old man! Come out here at once and help me withstand this fuss."

Mary Beth said, "Leonard, Teddy would like you to join us for breakfast."

"No such thing," Teddy said. "I need the emotional support is all. An objective third party to provide some—"

"You've got your napkin wrong," the little boy observed, sliding onto a chair at the table.

"I've got what?"

"Mom says we always put our napkins on our laps. You wanna be *polite*, don'tcha?"

Mary Beth started to speak, but Teddy said, "Fine objective third party you are, Leonard. If a man were to listen to you, he'd end up absolutely covered with marmalade. And I scarcely think you'd find *that* so polite—when I'd gotten sticky-orange from head to toe. Now then, do we engage in any type of morning devotionals before eggs, or not?"

Evidently the thought of Teddy's being all sticky-orange struck Leonard funny, because he began giggling until, out of control, he dissolved in a positive fit of laughter. While the boy was doubled over, and without waiting for an answer to the devotional question, Teddy took it upon himself to say grace:

"For Mary Beth and me and Leonard too—
Who's giggling at this very moment—Lord
Please bless this food. And bless your
            servant Carl

As well. We wish that he were with us.
Amen."

"You haven't changed a bit," Mary Beth said, not really wanting to hear about Carl.

"Of course I have," Teddy replied. "I'm an insufferable old man—getting crankier by the day."

Leonard stopped laughing and said, "I *do* wish Dad were here, Mom."

Mary Beth thought: He needs a haircut. And she turned her face from the table. "Please eat your breakfast," she said.

II

It had been a bitter divorce—one of those that starts out with an uncomplicated, if somewhat naive, decision on the part of the principals to separate, to be equitable, to remain friends, and ends up in this (for everyone involved) almost unbelievable, raw-emotion property dispute and custody battle.

Leonard was four when the roof caved in, so to speak, on his parents' marriage. He weathered the storm quite well, Mary Beth often said, and as a matter of fact, understood more than you might think. She didn't actually believe this, but it had a light-hearted ring, and repeating it kept her from screaming when acquaintances asked how the child was *managing*.

Carl took an apartment in Manhattan and visited Leonard on alternate weekends, until finally (with the court's imprimatur) Mary Beth moved herself, her allocated portion of the worldly goods, and their son to Boston—that haven of security where she had grown up and her parents still resided.

A disturbing incident occurred just after they arrived at this "new home"—which represented, for Leonard anyway, an island of painful, undeserved exile—and it happened at a large family gathering. Overcome by a sudden burst of creativity, Leonard decided to inform everyone—including Mary Beth's parents—that Carl had been imprisoned for armed robbery. Before Mary Beth could stop him or explain that he was making it *up*, for God's sake, he said the reason his father was not with them was because a judge in New York had put him *away*. To the present day Mary Beth had chosen not to think about the blasted implications of Leonard's announcement. At best, it made the muscles in her neck tight. Even without interpretation, however, the memory of that experience served continually to remind her of how the child *was* managing.

Teddy, on the other hand (and it should be noted that he was no casual bystander), seemed to have maintained his usual good humor and accepting nature throughout the recent turmoil. This in contrast to Mary Beth's parents, who never once tired of talking about how *they* had been simply *demolished* by the whole business. Furthermore, her mother and father said Teddy was a peculiar old man—the more so for having undertaken the rearing (some thirty years ago) of a seven-year-old orphan. Nor had they been above suggesting that the reasons behind the divorce, *etc.*, were

somehow linked to Teddy's having been a surrogate—
guardian or whatever it was called—for Carl, who (as
far as they were concerned) manifested abundant evi-
dence of being good and peculiar himself.

Mary Beth didn't agree with her parents. She had
even corresponded with Teddy from time to time dur-
ing the two years following the move. But she had
never before invited him to visit her and Leonard in
Boston. And if the truth were to be known, she couldn't
really say what prompted her to extend the invitation
now. Not that she didn't like having Teddy around. She
did. In fact, there were moments when Mary Beth felt
she had always known him. What disturbed her was
that vaguely religious quality of his. And the honesty of
course.

III

"Why don't we give Carl a call?" Teddy asked one
evening. He had earlier brought Leonard back from a
trip to the New England Aquarium. Now he was, to all
appearances at least, zealously working his way through
a month-old copy of *Newsweek*.

"I don't think that would be such a terribly good
idea right this instant," Mary Beth said, lighting her
first cigarette of the day. "I really don't." From another
room came the sound of an enthusiastic television com-
mercial.

"It might do everyone an absolute world of good,"
he replied, still turning pages.

"And you can keep on reading till you're blind,

Teddy! I am not—do you understand me—*not* talking with Carl."

He put down the magazine. "Who said anything about your talking? All I said was, let's give him a call."

"Look, Teddy. You aren't just suddenly wanting to phone Carl without—"

"I am too! I call him every now and then when you're not even *there*. And I certainly never say: Carl, here's Mary Beth on the line wanting to talk with you. I mean, why would I? You're miles away in Boston. I'd have to be crazy to do something like that. Besides, I promised Leonard—"

"You promised Leonard?"

"I did. We were standing by a drinking fountain, if I remember correctly, when Leonard said he would like to phone his father and could we do that later tonight. Naturally, I said we could—not wishing, there and then, to shatter the child's day."

"Teddy, listen to me for a minute—"

"He wanted to know if Carl goes to lots of singles' bars. He said he saw a television show about—"

"*What?*"

"Singles' bars. You know, the kind of place where people get together for—"

"My God! Teddy, do you know what you're saying?"

"I didn't ask *him*, Mary Beth. He asked me. And yes, I believe I know what I'm saying. At least there's *that* about me. I'm hardly senile—just a bit fragile and infirm. The mind continues to hum right along."

"Well that does it!" Mary Beth said, imploring the

ceiling for understanding. "That honestly *does* it! Leonard wants to know if Carl goes to lots of—did he say lots of? Obviously that's what he said. *Lots* of singles' bars! I'm surprised he hasn't asked my *mother* about Carl's sex life. I mean it. That honestly does it for me, Teddy. I'm a total failure."

"You're not a failure," Teddy said. "And Leonard asked a perfectly legitimate question. He's curious, that's all. As a matter of fact, I'm sort of curious myself. However, it isn't nearly *killing* me to think about it—"

"I suppose you think maybe it's killing *me*? That I sit around picturing Carl in some afterhours dive— sweet talking this Fifth Avenue fashion model bimbo who, in her spare time mind you, just simply *lives* for the theater and totally *adores* Genet's complexity—"

"The thought had crossed my mind, yes," Teddy said. "You know, Mary Beth, wonderful, miraculous things happen to people when they're my age. For instance, I can say almost anything I please—and get away with it. Those who agree assume the years have made me wise. Those who take exception dismiss the comments as having been made by a doddering old fool. Either way, I get to express what's on my mind and that's a luxury few enjoy. For example: *I* think we should give Carl a call and ask him about that Fifth Avenue bimbo."

"Teddy, you *are* a doddering old fool! I was only imagining the scene because we started talking about singles' bars."

"There it is—the first sign of abuse! Am I to be the subject of continuing verbal attack—merely because of my advanced years? Whatever possessed you to call a fine elderly gentleman like myself a doddering old fool?"

"You're impossible!"

"I know—because I like marmalade. And now a doddering old fool for offering sound advice to a stubborn, lonely young woman who won't pay attention even to the anguished cries of her only son—"

"Will you stop this carrying on if we make the call?"

"You won't hear a peep from me. Not another word, I swear. It would seem far too much like meddling. Besides, I've already caused enough stir—and that without actually saying a thing, I might add. I simply reported what Leonard told me and suggested that you honor the child's wishes to talk with his father."

"Hah!"

"Hah, indeed! Did I once mention the article I was reading in *Newsweek* about how an astonishing number of divorced couples end up remarrying *each other*? I did not. It also gave a good deal of rationale—which by the way I found to be quite insightful and compelling. But did I attempt to foist off this brilliant analysis—?"

"There's no such article, Teddy. And what's more, you're doing it again right now. You're carrying on." Mary Beth finished her cigarette.

"Well, the article said most people have some excellent reasons for getting together in the first place, you know. And after a certain length of time apart,

there often comes a clearer intellectual understanding
of what was once an intuitive reaching out—"

"I happen to *know* there's no such article in that
magazine—"

Leonard burst into the room, dragging a torn and
somewhat grimy comforter behind him. "Didja ask her
yet, Teddy?" came the question at top volume. "Didja?"

IV

"Hello?" Teddy said into the phone. A younger
man's voice—filled with affectionate recognition—came
to life at the other end. "Wait a minute! Is this some
kind of crank call?"

"Getting crankier every day," Teddy said, grimac-
ing at Mary Beth. "It happens to old people, you
know—"

"Who is this *really*?" Carl carried on the familiar
routine.

"Can't speak to that right this minute because
tempus fugit, if you know what I mean, you no good
rascal! For the time being, why don't we just say I'm an
ancient emissary who, by one means or another, man-
aged to get your number?"

"You know how I *hate* crank calls, Teddy!"

"Please! Spare me your idiosyncrasies. I have here
in the room with me two perfectly nice people virtually
overflowing with questions for you. It is *my* mission

merely to obtain your ear. And to make certain you do not avoid—as has been your somewhat annoying custom—the real issues at stake."

"Are you in Boston? Teddy, you're in Boston, aren't you? What in blazes do you think you're *doing* anyway? I mean it, old trooper—you're in Boston, aren't you? You just decided to take a trip, or what? Listen—is everything all right? Nobody's *hurt* or anything like that—"

"Not at all. Leonard simply wants to know about the singles' bars you go to," Teddy said, waving Mary Beth back from a wild attempt to seize the phone.

"What singles' bars?"

"And Mary Beth wants you to provide the lurid details on that fashion model you've been seeing."

"Teddy, have you been drinking?"

"Not yet," Teddy said, while Mary Beth glowered at him. "I'm presently on a rather ticklish assignment that requires full-tilt use of what remaining faculties I possess."

"Assignment?"

"Look, Carl, I'm going to hand the phone to Mary Beth now. You got that? Just be sure to ask her about the really fascinating article she's been reading in *Newsweek*—will you do that for me? No kidding. It tells how divorce affects the male partner—did you know, some men actually *believe* the nonsense society hands out about their being the strong ones? And then they end up even more alone and afraid—"

Mary Beth lunged for the phone. This time she

was successful. "Carl?" she said, her voice filled with emotion.

V

You should never meddle like that, you old fool, Teddy thought as he flicked the light switch on before going upstairs. Oh hogwash, came his own inner reply—you've only got one life to live—why not live dangerously? From the study he could hear Leonard's frantic voice: "Lemme talk to him! Lemme *talk* to him!"

He was aware that he ought to have said goodnight or something of the sort, but under the circumstances it had seemed a bit like overkill. This business of tinkering with historical events was tiring though, and with or without the usual amenities, Teddy recognized bedtime when he saw it.

There were, in all, sixteen carpeted stairs to climb. Hardly like running to the top of the Empire State Building, Teddy smiled—remembering another place, another time. But for now it was enough. Not that the ascent represented a more than normally hazardous undertaking. It was just that—after an evening of perilous meddling—he felt like being extra careful. So when upon reaching the eighth stair he experienced a slight tightness in the chest, it caused him to stop for a moment. A little reminder of mortality, he thought. And he grasped the handrail more firmly than before.

But the sensation did not pass immediately. After a few seconds came increased tightness and shooting pain that seemed to radiate from sternum to esophagus, across the left shoulder, and down that arm. He thought: Careful, Mister, or they'll never invite *you* again. Then, although he remained standing upright, it suddenly felt like someone was sitting full force on his chest. No pain to speak of—just lots and lots of pressure. "Not good," he said half-aloud, turned, and sat down where he was.

Because he was having such trouble breathing, he loosened his tie and pulled the collar open. He kept expecting to lose consciousness. The sweat covering his forehead and soaking through his shirt scared him. He thought: I suppose if I die right here, Leonard will be the one to find me. Talk about being *scared*. He fervently wished it would not be Leonard—and while he was wishing that, he began to shiver.

Then a miracle happened. At least, as far as Teddy was concerned it was a miracle. The pressure eased, the radiating pain stopped, and the tightness went away—all while he continued shivering. In truth, the more he shivered, the better he felt. And *that* scared him too—only in a good way this time—and it made him shiver the more—until his teeth fairly rattled with relief.

"Whatcha doing, Teddy?" Leonard asked, peering up at him.

"Well, I'm sh-shivering, Leonard," he said. And he had never before been so happy to tell anyone anything.

MATTER OF TIME

Words and Music by
Martin Bell

Vi-sions of a time___ that used to be___
help me find a rea - son to be-lieve in you.
I've been do - ing fine___ as you can see. I've
found my-self a room___ to use as a re - treat.___
___ It's a mat-ter of time.___

CHORUS

Some-thing's ven - tured.___ Some-thing is gained.

Giv- en time_ our love_ must change. But time __ is nev-er
giv - en _____ on - ly tak - en or re - ar - ranged.

MATTER OF TIME

1. Visions of a time that used to be
   Help me find a reason to believe in you.
   I've been doing fine—as you can see.
   I've found myself a room to use as a retreat.
   It's a matter of time.

   Truth cannot be measured; that's a limitation.
   We spend the night together, but love has no
       duration.
   It never could begin or end in time at all.
   And losing you has hurt me.
   It's a matter of time.

   > *Something's ventured. Something is gained.*
   > *Given time, our love must change.*
   > *But time is never given—*
   > *Only taken or rearranged.*

2. The child inside me crying has stepped into the fire
   Of once upon a time and found it was required
   That he sign away his birthright—the claim to his
       confusion.
   And time has made him tired of my seclusion.
   It's a matter of time.

   I remember how it was when you were mine.
   I never took you—only borrowed what I could
       and left the rest.

And now I think of you at night. Well, the truth
    is that I need you more than sleep.
And on the ceiling are the shadows of my memories.
It's a matter of time.

> *Something's ventured. Something is gained.*
> *Given time, our love must change.*
> *But time is never given—*
> *Only taken or rearranged.*

Sweeping Meditations #12 & 17

[yielding]
#12

You and I are complex
bundles of energy,
related to each other
in curious ways.
The positive and
negative polarities
make life possible.

We live in tension: stretched out between hope for gracious providence and a corresponding call to—REPENT.

God entrusts
fallible, rebellious
individuals
with the glorious
carrying-out of his purpose.

The Word
is hurled at us
like a stone.
And, enabled by
that announcement, each of us
ventures forth into the world
as a hopeful, missional
storyteller.

Nothing goes without saying.

Jesus said: You are free from the bondage of your own condemnation. Free to live. Free to decide. Your sins are forgiven. And this is how you will know that you are free. Forgive one another and yourself—even as I have forgiven you.

God's judgment is the same as His mercy.

In other words, He will not let us go to hell in peace.

We are not victims. We are not guests.

You and I are colleagues and co-creators with Him— living in the midst of ongoing creation and called upon to celebrate everything that is.

Because, for God, everything that is, is necessary— and received.

Therefore, being thankful means saying *yes* to life, in spite of all the obvious suffering, brokenness, and guilt.

To give thanks is to have the courage to get up in the morning.

Life is worth the dying.

And faith has to do with:
   —passionate commitment balanced against stark
      humility.
   —openness to miracles in everyday occurrence.
   —affirmation of co-responsibility for creating
      what will be.
Faith drives us from intensely personal existence
into the raw stuff of historical encounter.

There's no such thing as
a we-self or group
consciousness.

Individuals must think,
weigh up, and decide.

You just can't rely on
someone else's faith.

At the core of everyone is a unique and wonderful
vision—a way of perceiving shared by no other crea-
ture. However, each of us also inherits a second-hand
social universe—

an organizing principle,   I didn't know the
architectural design,   question before I
elemental philosophy,   learned the answer.
if you will—which
imperceptibly becomes yet another part of the total
life-map.

In truth, though, what you see
is *not* what you get.

Sooner or later, that social universe
                              is going to break
                              under data-strain.
Then what will
remain?

                    Sounds,
                    visions,
                    insights,
                    questions,
                    exploding—
                              light.

Here's looking at you, kid.

Education is the process
by which individuals
teach themselves.

Give up sainthood before it's too late!
Empty yourself of everything.
Subtle, mysterious, profound, responsive—
God is ruthless.

Consider the lilies of the field.

[centering]
#17

It's always difficult to
begin a conversation.
Looking into the
unknown
of another
person, I don't
know what to expect.

There are as many universes
as there are people.

Coming to terms with human finitude is the beginning
of wisdom. And by wisdom, one learns to celebrate
Mystery, and in so doing, a person grasps after the One
who guarantees that *things never work out the way we
plan*—the One who offers no explanations whatsoever.

There's a piece of   Who's in charge here?
the puzzle missing!
                             Not by searching.
                             Not by waiting.

You and I are not in this place by our own design, nor
have we come without reservations. I, for one, am
caught by the grinding wheel of history; lost in a laby-
rinth of doubt; traveling blind, trusting the wind.

Life comes to me
as a series of encounters
with Mystery.

[Unfathomable depths?
Not this! Not that!]

Before there was anything, there was nothing.
Later, in a world of boundless acoustic space,
human intellect perceived *now* and *then*.

For some reason, we are
creatures who love to mea-
sure. And reason (for some)
is the backbone of human
knowledge. They say it is
the most excellent tool we
have yet devised.

But then, for what *reason*
are utterly new creatures
still emerging from the
immeasurable bog?

Revelation means getting a peek at
the reality that is always there.

It's all one.
It's all one.

As a matter of fact, *things never work out the way we plan.* SOMETHING always interrupts.

> Every
> answer
> questioned.

Eternal legend—here and now—permeates the matrix of historical situation. That is to say, the tables are turned on time and space.

God raises Jesus from the dead.
He is alive today.

Chronology (basis for the whole cause-and-effect nexus) has ended. *Kairos* (God's high time) is upon us.

> [Three good reasons for
> Resurrection?
> Not this! Not that!]

By way of response to the Christ, a person is either converted or offended. Of course, some are both converted *and* offended.

It's the real thing.

A Word shatters illusion.
It says: There is no
security. There is only
Holy Insecurity.

Sweeping aside the admonitions of those who suggest,
implore, even demand that he stay on the mountaintop,
Jesus resolutely sets his face toward Jerusalem.

No time left.

Strangely, all of what
you do depends on who
you think you are.

Just who do you think
you are anyway?

You are everyone who ever was
and everyone who ever will be.

Decisions that you make in what we call this present—
this here and now—will validate (or invalidate) every-

thing that has gone before, and make possible (or impossible) all that is yet to come.

> This is your moment—
>> your special time to proclaim . . .

The Story
first whispered against a backdrop of noise and sweat
    and confusion;
later shouted into long, silent corridors
    of hope;
and finally carried to the furthest limits
    of awareness—
even unto the realm we call eternity.

The Story
told by those who honestly confront their humanity,
see the nightmare and the dream, and refuse
    to look away.
told in the manifold languages of computers
    and world politics;
the incisive imagery of drama and film;
the wild, free, revealing expressions of music;
and in the poignant, even revolutionary,
    idiom of sacred worship.

To be seized by the
living God is a fierce   Business as usual
and terrible and   sort of falls
beautiful thing.   by the wayside.

A great silver wolf
growls at the desert.

Bethlehem, Occupied West Bank (AP)—

The whole of the created universe has been
breathlessly anticipating your arrival.

History is on the move!

Earth
Fire
Air
Water

"If you don't have a plan,
how will you know whether
or not you're winning?"
—Western technologist

"Take everything
as it comes—
don't plan ahead."
—Oriental pirate

Enough is enough
and
too much is never enough.

Scriptural Themes

Now faith is the assurance of things hoped for, the conviction of things not seen. For by it the men of old received divine approval. By faith we understand that the world was created by the word of God, so that what is seen was made out of things which do not appear. *Hebrews 11:1–3*

But we have this treasure in earthen vessels, to show that the transcendent power belongs to God and not to us. We are afflicted in every way, but not crushed; perplexed, but not driven to despair; persecuted, but not forsaken; struck down, but not destroyed; always carrying in the body the death of Jesus, so that the life of Jesus may also be manifested in our bodies. For while we live we are always being given up to death for Jesus' sake, so that the life of Jesus may be manifested in our mortal flesh. *II Corinthians 4:7–11*

Put on the whole armor of God, that you may be able to stand against the wiles of the devil. For we are not contending against flesh and blood, but against the principalities, against the powers, against the world rulers of this present darkness, against the spiritual hosts of wickedness in the heavenly places. *Ephesians 6:11–12*

Behold I go forward, but he is not there,
And backward, but I cannot perceive him;
On the left hand I seek him, but I cannot behold him;
I turn to the right hand, but I cannot see him.
But he knows the way that I take.

Job 23:8–10

He reached from on high, he took me,
    he drew me out of many waters.
He delivered me from my strong enemy,
    and from those who hated me;
    for they were too mighty for me.

Psalm 18:16–17

Jesus said to her, "Every one who drinks of this water will thirst again, but whoever drinks of the water that I shall give him will never thirst; the water that I shall give him will become in him a spring of water welling up to eternal life." *John 4:13–14*

And in that region there were shepherds out in the field, keeping watch over their flock by night. And an angel of the Lord appeared to them, and the glory of the Lord shone around them, and they were filled with fear. And the angel said to them, "Be not afraid; for behold, I bring you good news of a great joy which will come to all the people; for to you is born this day in the city of David a Savior, who is Christ the Lord. And this will be a sign for you: you will find a babe wrapped in swaddling cloths and lying in a manger." *Luke 2:8–12*

The earth is the Lord's and the fulness thereof,
    the world and those who dwell therein;
for he has founded it upon the seas,
    and established it upon the rivers, . . .
Lift up your heads, O gates!
    and be lifted up, O ancient doors!
    that the King of glory may come in.
Who is the King of glory?
    The Lord, strong and mighty,
    The Lord, mighty in battle!
Lift up your heads, O gates!
    and be lifted up, O ancient doors!
    that the King of glory may come in.
Who is this King of glory?
    The Lord of hosts,
    he is the King of glory!

Psalm 24:1–2, 7–10

And now men cannot look on the light
    when it is bright in the skies,
    when the wind has passed and cleared them.
Out of the north comes golden spendor;
    God is clothed with terrible majesty.

Job 37:21–22

    Be patient, therefore, brethren, until the coming
of the Lord. Behold, the farmer waits for the precious
fruit of the earth, being patient over it until it receives
the early and the late rain. You also be patient. Estab-
lish your hearts, for the coming of the Lord is at hand.
Do not grumble, brethren, against one another, that

you may not be judged; behold the Judge is standing at the doors. As an example of suffering and patience, brethren, take the prophets who spoke in the name of the Lord. *James 5:7–10*

Be watchful, stand firm in your faith, be courageous, be strong. Let all that you do be done in love. *I Corinthians 16:13–14*

None of us lives to himself, and none of us dies to himself. If we live, we live to the Lord, and if we die, we die to the Lord; so then, whether we live or whether we die, we are the Lord's. For to this end Christ died and lived again, that he might be the Lord both of the dead and of the living. *Romans 14:7–9*

Do not be conformed to this world but be transformed by the renewal of your mind, that you may prove what is the will of God, what is good and acceptable and perfect. *Romans 12:2*

Now the word of the Lord came to Jonah the son of Amittai, saying, "Arise, go to Nineveh, that great city, and cry against it; for their wickedness has come up before me." But Jonah rose to flee to Tarshish from the presence of the Lord. *Jonah 1:1–3*

Moses said to the Lord, "Oh, my Lord, I am not eloquent, either heretofore or since thou hast spoken to thy servant; but I am slow of speech and of tongue." Then the Lord said to him, "Who has made man's mouth? Who makes him dumb, or deaf, or seeing, or blind? Is it not I, the Lord? Now therefore go, and I will be with your mouth and teach you what you shall speak." *Exodus 4:10–12*

Now the word of the Lord came to me saying, "Before I formed you in the womb I knew you, and before you were born I consecrated you; I appointed you a prophet to the nations." Then I said, "Ah, Lord God! Behold, I do not know how to speak, for I am only a youth." But the Lord said to me, "Do not say, 'I am only a youth'; for to all to whom I send you you shall go, and whatever I command you you shall speak. Be not afraid of them, for I am with you to deliver you, says the Lord." *Jeremiah 1:4–8*

Then the Spirit lifted me up and took me away, and I went in bitterness in the heat of my spirit, the hand of the Lord being strong upon me. *Ezekiel 3:14*

And I said: "Woe is me! For I am lost; for I am a man of unclean lips, and I dwell in the midst of a people of unclean lips; for my eyes have seen the King, the Lord of hosts!" Then flew one of the seraphim to me, having in his hand a burning coal which he had taken with tongs from the altar. And he touched my mouth, and said: "Behold, this has touched your lips; your guilt is taken away, and your sin forgiven." And I heard the voice of the Lord saying, "Whom shall I send, and who will go for us?" Then I said, "Here am I! Send me." *Isaiah 6:5–8*

As he went, the people pressed round him. And a woman who had had a flow of blood for twelve years and could not be healed by any one, came up behind him, and touched the fringe of his garment; and immediately her flow of blood ceased. And Jesus said, "Who was it that touched me?" When all denied it, Peter said, "Master, the multitudes surround you and press upon you!" But Jesus said, "Some one touched me; for I perceive that power has gone forth from me." And when the woman saw that she was not hidden, she came trembling, and falling down before him declared in the presence of all the people why she had touched him, and how she had been immediately healed. And he said to her, "Daughter, your faith has made you well; go in peace." *Luke 8:42b–48*

And they came to Jesus, and saw the demoniac sitting there, clothed and in his right mind, the man who had had the legion; and they were afraid. And those who had seen it told what had happened to the demoniac and to the swine. And they began to beg Jesus to depart from their neighborhood. And as he was getting into the boat, the man who had been possessed with demons begged him that he might be with him. But he refused, and said to him, "Go home to your friends, and tell them how much the Lord has done for you, and how he has had mercy on you." *Mark 5:15–19*

Beloved, do not be surprised at the fiery ordeal which comes upon you to prove you, as though something strange were happening to you. But rejoice in so far as you share Christ's sufferings, that you may also rejoice and be glad when his glory is revealed. *I Peter 4:12–13*

Rejoice always, pray constantly; give thanks in all circumstances; for this is the will of God in Christ Jesus for you. *I Thessalonians 5:16–18*

In this is love, not that we loved God but that he loved us and sent his Son to be the expiation for our sins. Beloved, if God so loved us, we also ought to love one another. No man has ever seen God; if we love one another, God abides in us and his love is perfected in us. *I John 4:10–12*

"Therefore I tell you, do not be anxious about your life, what you shall eat or what you shall drink, nor about your body, what you shall put on. Is not life more than food, and the body more than clothing? Look at the birds of the air: they neither sow nor reap nor gather into barns, and yet your heavenly Father feeds them. Are you not of more value than they? And which of you by being anxious can add one cubit to his span of life? And why are you anxious about clothing? Consider the lilies of the field, how they grow; they neither toil nor spin; yet I tell you, even Solomon in all his glory was not arrayed like one of these." *Matthew 6:25–29*